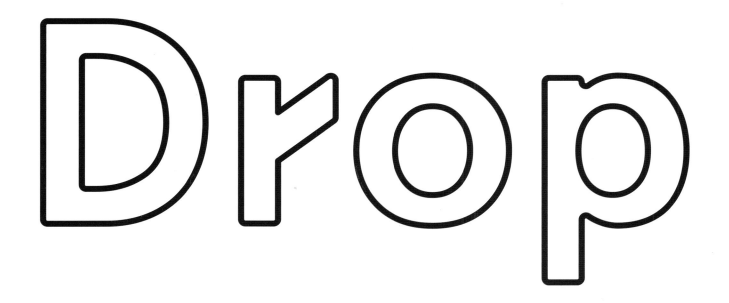

Drop

Vetements

A Bathing Ape

Supreme

The Life of Pablo

Palace

Anti Social Social Club

Off-White

Gosha Rubchinskiy

VLONE

Rick Owens

InkLaw

OriginalFake

Uniqlo

Louis Vuitton

Kinfolk

fragment design

Yeezy

Dover Street Market

Brooklyn, NY

Foreword

As if 2017 couldn't get any weirder, Bizarro World appears fully booked until further notice. So what the fuck happened to streetwear?

For better or worse, the once niche realm of drops and exclusive products has firmly crossed over to the other side. The faint sliver of overlap between the disparate world of streetwear and high fashion has become a full-fledged amalgamation, a mutant genre in and of itself.

And the dollars keep pouring in.

Subculture is now the culture and an accepted, highly-emulated one at that. Sure, there have always been biters, but never has capital-F *Fashion* so shamelessly worn its inspiration on its sleeve. Show me any point in history when the major houses were so keen to go slumming it at the street level.

Look no further than every fragmented collection with multiple releases throughout the season, limited edition collaboration, and youth culture-oriented activation dominating the headlines from *GQ* to *Vogue*. Cultural appropriation is the trend du jour.

Where should you send your strongly worded letter, or edible arrangement, depending on how much your butt hurts? See: the Internet. Our ability to interact with the entire world at any given time has utterly recodified every possible parameter of every industry, including fashion. We speak to strangers from all over the globe more comfortably than our next door neighbors. Shared interests and experiences exist entirely independently of geography. It's pretty fucking sweet, right? Well, maybe for some. Either way, the kids indoctrinating each other on the intricacies of T-shirts are using identical avenues as the too-cool-for-school old heads lambasting those very same kids for giving a shit about garments produced before they were even a glimmer in their dad's nuts. Unfortunately, this irony is more often than not lost on the kind of person willing to pay $100 for a sticker.

Welcome to the New World. Supreme used to be for skaters. AF1s were the purview of the court. People would mission to other cities hunting special editions. No more. The products and marketplace have become culturally and geo-agnostic. And business is booming. streetwear might not quite be the new heroin, but, on any given Thursday, there's a line of kids waiting outside the stash house.

5

13

Drop

15

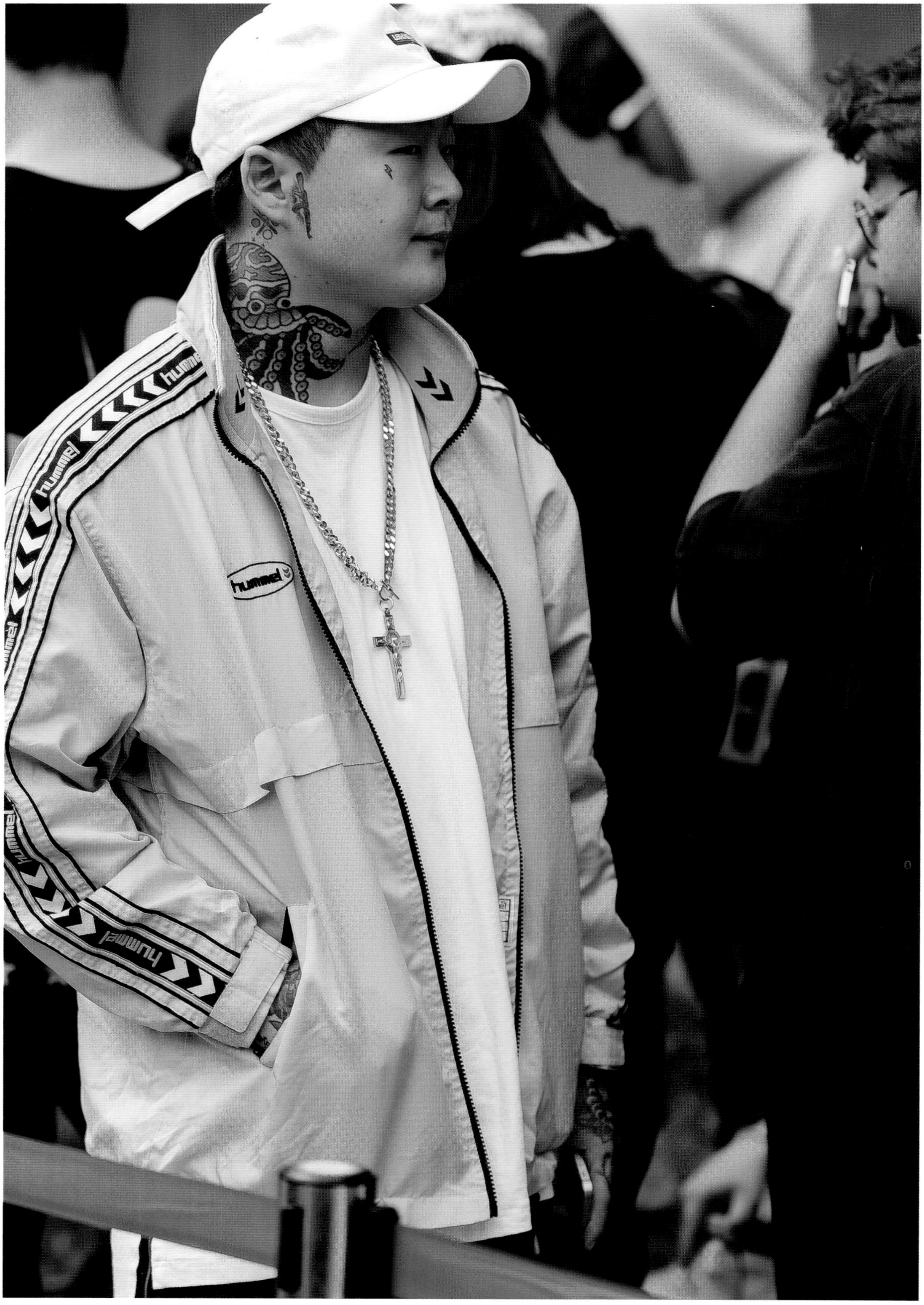
hummel

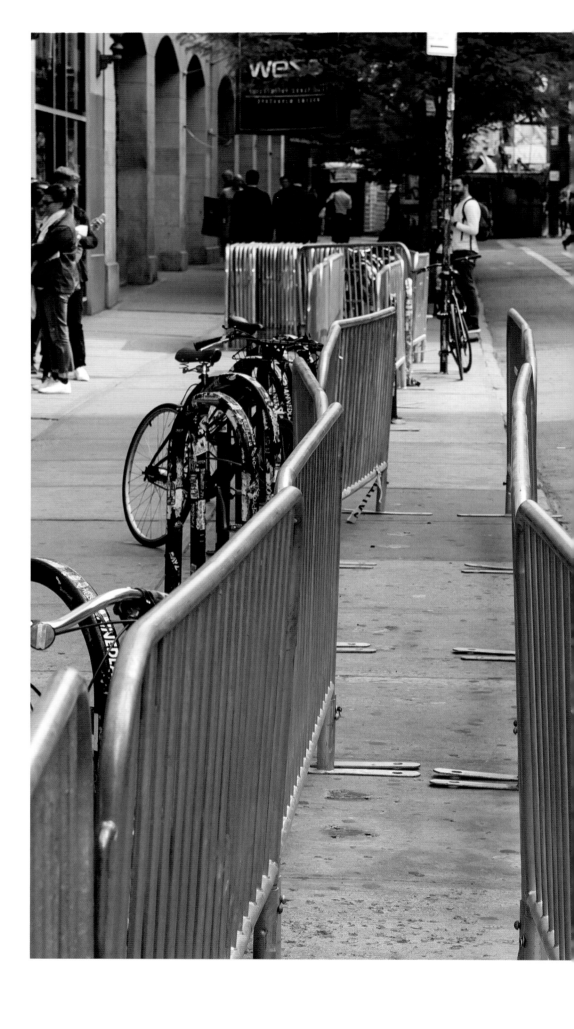

A rai... ...ot) or slicker is ...waterproof or water-resistant coat worn to protect the body from rain. The term rain jacket is sometimes ...sed to refer to raincoa...that are waist length. A rain jacket may be combi...d with a pair of rain p...s to make a rain suit.

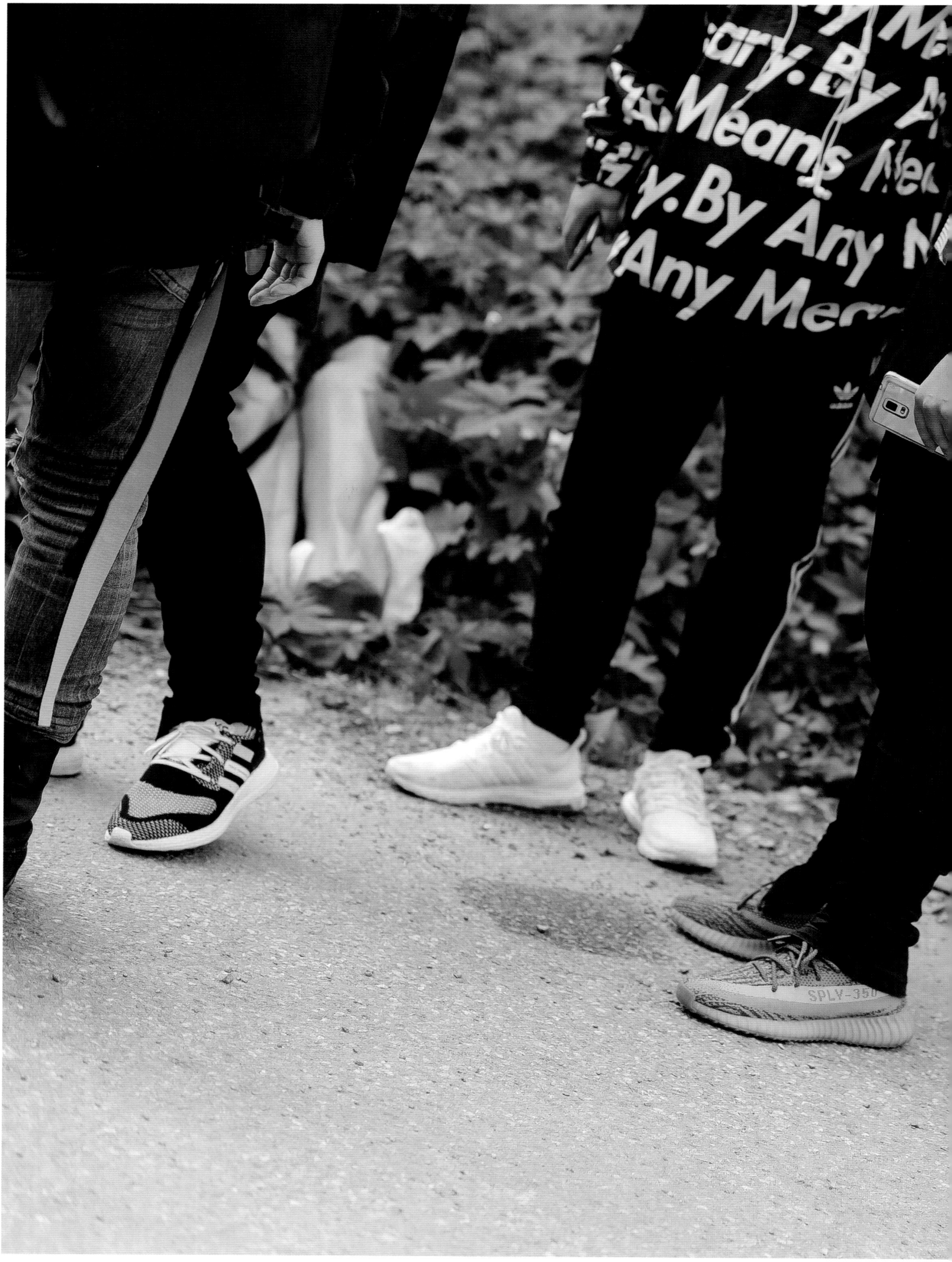
Means
By Any

45

57

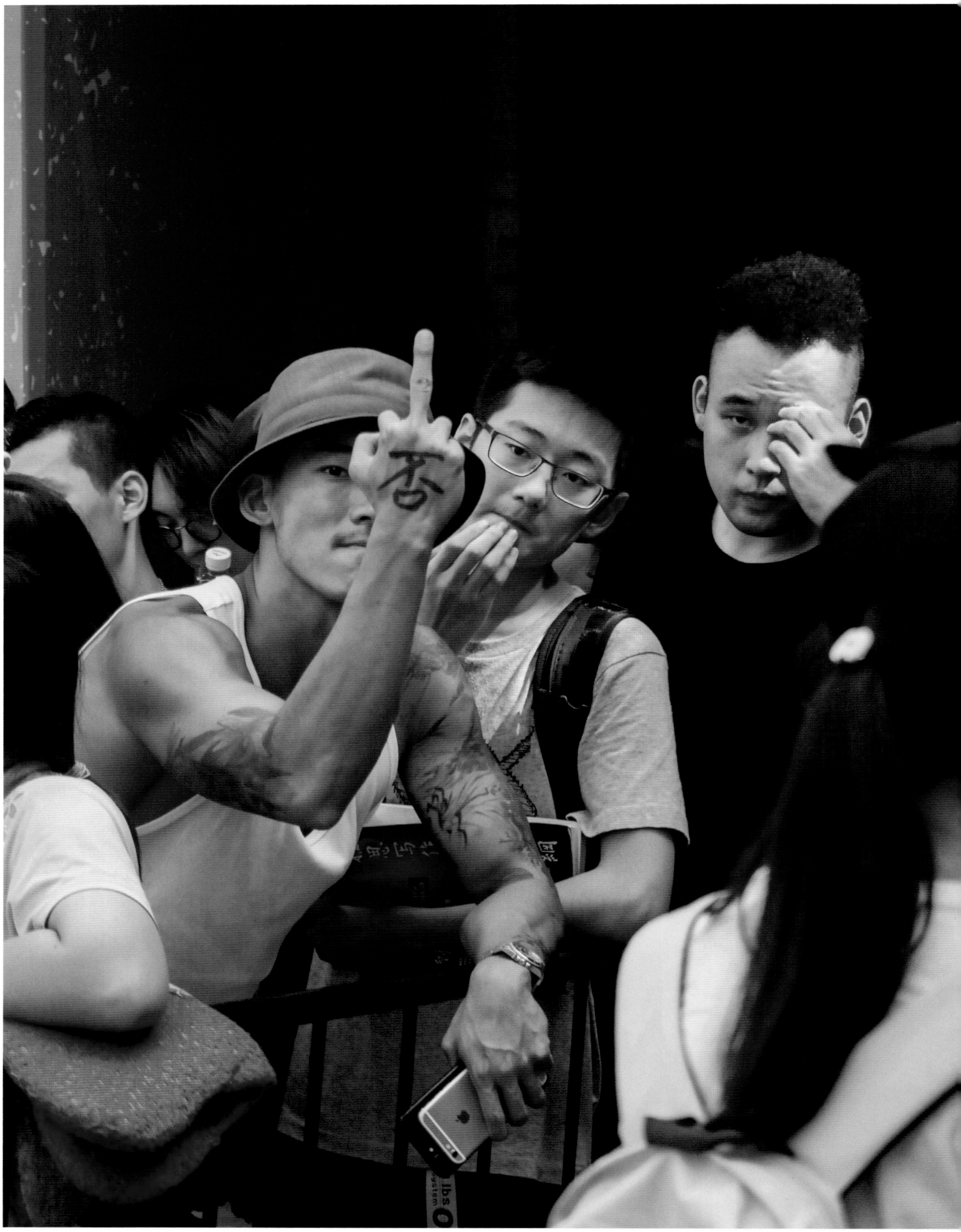

Reflecting on the evolution of the streetwear world is a sobering proposition. One only has to pop open the dog-eared first edition of *Where'd You Get Those* that any true head has on their shelf, to realize how much yesterday is not like today.

This may age me, but I remember missioning to other cities for limited edition drops. 6-training uptown for a release that just wasn't happening south of 110th Street. Hitting up the homie who had a cousin in Philly (or wherever) and trying to figure out what tradables I had that would con-vince a stranger to get in line for a pair of kicks that seemed no more special than any others in their mind.

Streetwear was, then, a whispered pursuit. An inclusive community of like-minded otaku. 90s Gundam figurine fan goonies who probably got laid. And would lay that slice of plain cheese right on your face if you half-stepped.

It didn't have gods, it had prophets. Bobbito, high upon the mountaintop. Tinker, taking a trip of three steps down the palate to tap, at three, on the teeth. Michael, tongue wagging, chaste in his naked competitiveness. A pre-TMZ virgin of peak iconography. Before a single fuxk was given about how our legends lived their lives behind closed doors.

As the poet said, things done changed. Now, there be gods. Ye wielding a trident; Poseidon plumbing those murky depths. Virgil reposing, resplendently, Botticelli-esque, atop a cloud. Ronnie Fieg as Dionysus; throwing an endless party of playful homage/badinage, replete with (cherry) Coke. Neek playing Puck, flashing 22s in a one-time-only performance of *A Midsummer Night's Fever Dream.*

Then sites like eBay and Grailed changed the game. Now it's about spending, not politicking. Everything is in reach of that Black Card. There's advantages and disadvantages to this. OGs sit around lamenting that the game is dead. But that's kinda what OGs do. It's how they roll.

The streetwear world has also opened up to a whole new audience. And globalization can't just be about conglomerates exploiting labor costs in some far off banana republic. It also has to be about broader cultural promotion. Cool kids in Quito are fiending on Heron Preston; peeps in Hanoi are repping Off-White all day. I bumped into a kid in Soweto the other month rocking a tiger camo 'Preme bogo earflap five-panel. Talking about he copped two at Lafayette the one time he crossed an ocean, and gave one to a (now ex) girlfriend. Every couple weeks he considers calling her to see if he can get it back.

We all have the same stories. Alone. Together. Scrolling through the ether. Thirsting on Chrome.

And, let's be honest. Subcultures are no longer sub; *sous-groupe* is an anachronist myth. Much like *Fruits*-era Tokyo style, there's a series of readily identifiable street fashion tropes (which were laid out perfectly in the seminal tome *Fuck Yeah MensWear*—co-written by the author of this book's foreword, Lawrence Schlossman. The Down AF hypebeast, inevitably rocking those maroon Calabasas joggers and a Palace lightweight; the Street (Goth) Ninja, who thinks Rick wrote at least three of the Ten Commandments (thou will not covet thy neighbour's Ramones tho); the Egoist, who puts aside personal taste and will rock anything hot. You know the type. Sold his little sister's stamp collection to cop those Yeezy Zebras.

But the true shift in the streetwear world is that there's no longer a clearly definable streetwear world. Street fashion is fashion, and vice-versa. Rocky rucks Loewe. Donatella soundtracks Migos. There are no lines. This muhfucka straight ombré from here on out.

The lines between genres of clothing no longer exist. There are no more countercultures, only subcultures. Even the concept of subcultures, when examined in the dictionary, sounds more like advertising jargon than anything else. To wit: "Subculture: to cultivate a (bacterial) strain again on a new medium." Or: "The cultural values and behavioral patterns distinctive of a particular group in a society." Doesn't that kind of sound like it was written by Wieden+Kennedy, like they're referring to fucking memes? (Remember when that word followed us around like it was Kim and we were Kanye?)

The world of the hypebeast has led to a virtual destruction of the traditional delineation between street and high fashion. Limited edition pieces enjoy global cult status, draw thousands of hopeful purchasers, and can resell for up to 10-20x retail immediately after release on sites like Grailed. A couple months ago I saw a 50-something-year-old couple at the I.T. x Dover Street Market shop in Beijing. Not fashion people. Not creatives. Just obviously wealthy. He was stuffed into a Michele-era Gucci x Coco Capitán T-shirt, some Balmain bikers, and some chunky-ass Ricks. She was wearing some sort of CDG mumu and had an LV Supreme cross-body. The rules are different. The game has definitely changed. And a big part of that is the hype surrounding limited edition drops.

There is an entire culture surrounding these drops. Streetwear aficionados travel intercontinentally to attend them, almost like concerts, and wear their rarest shoes and gear, flexing for each other while chatting, comparing, and hoping to cop one-time-only pieces. Kids rock grails and geek out, like an OG subreddit come to life. Fuccboi Safari. Spot the creatures in their natural environment.

These days, these lines also represent some of the most interesting fashion events in the world, and are fast becoming streetwear's equivalent to the catwalk shows that haute ateliers host each year at fashion weeks in Paris, New York, Milan, and beyond.

But they're more and more drawing attention and scrutiny. Because when Balenciaga throws 10 million euros at an event, and everyone from Kate Moss to G-Dragon to Skateboard P shows up to rep the front row, there's a reasonable expectation of hype. The combination of talent, gloss, and Pinault's bank balance means that there will inevitably be more than a couple of eyeballs.

But when a company like Supreme is selling $44 T-shirts and drawing overnight queues, and resale gets so high that there's an entire industry of people making their living buying the hotness and reselling (saying nothing about shops like Round Two, Cop vs Drop, Unique Hype); trust that it's gonna make waves.

This is also not exactly the underground anymore. *Wired* did a 10-page feature on Supreme's cyber security. *GQ* regularly touts their wares. Dorothy, we've left the LES.

It's a foregone conclusion that Supreme's marketing hijinx will be the purview of a Wharton course sometime in the very near future. I mean, let's be real. 'Preme launches one box logo per year, and it's a RiRi secret show-level event. Resale prices instantly hit the stratosphere. And cats take notice.

For better or worse, the streetwear world will never be the same. But what we're trying to do with this book is catch a glimpse of the pureness. The cats who are out here. For the love. For the culture. For the daps.

"Yo, I like your kicks my man." From a stranger. Out of nowhere. That's what it's all about.

— Byron Hawes

71

101

103

Drop

Supreme

119

123

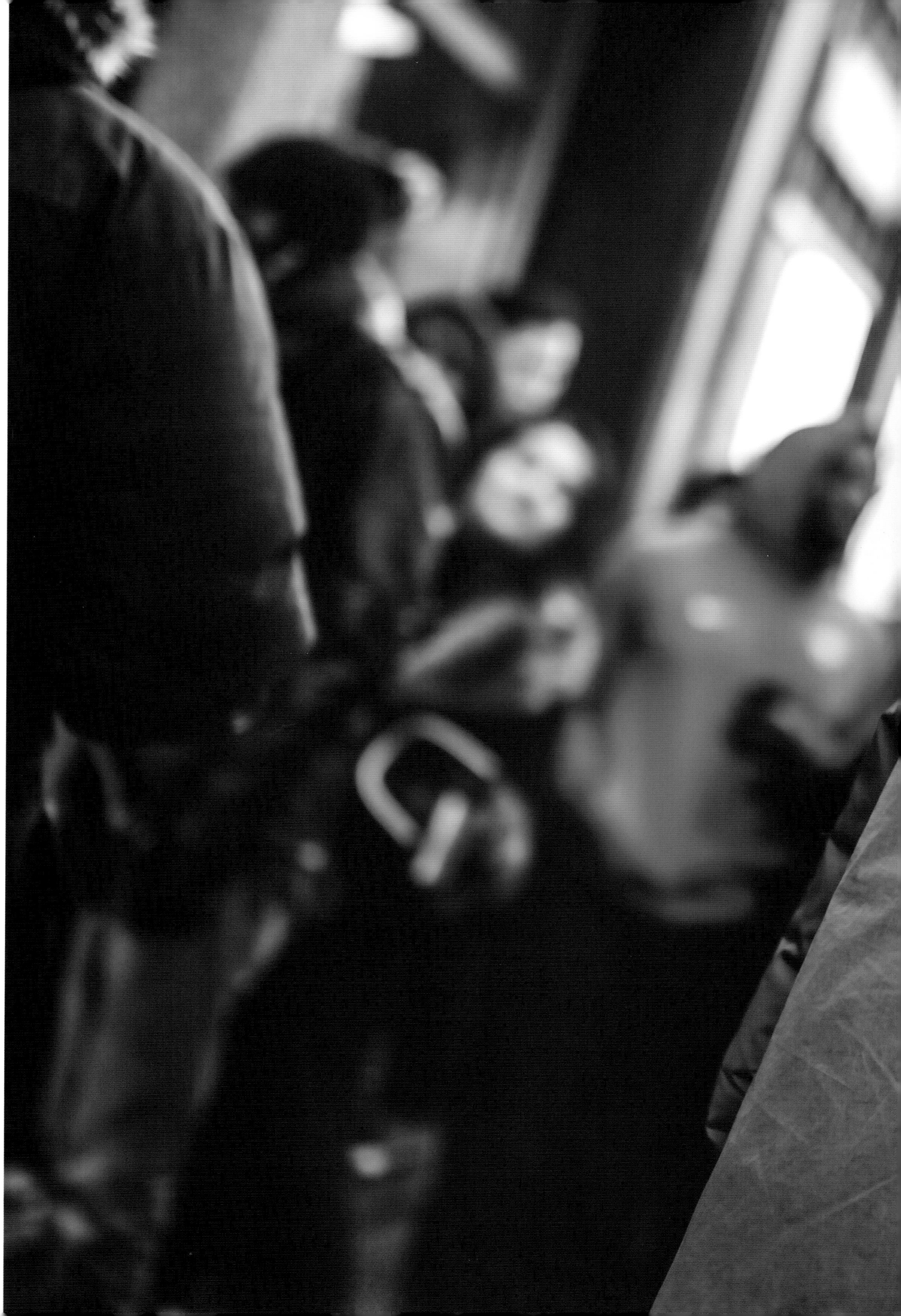

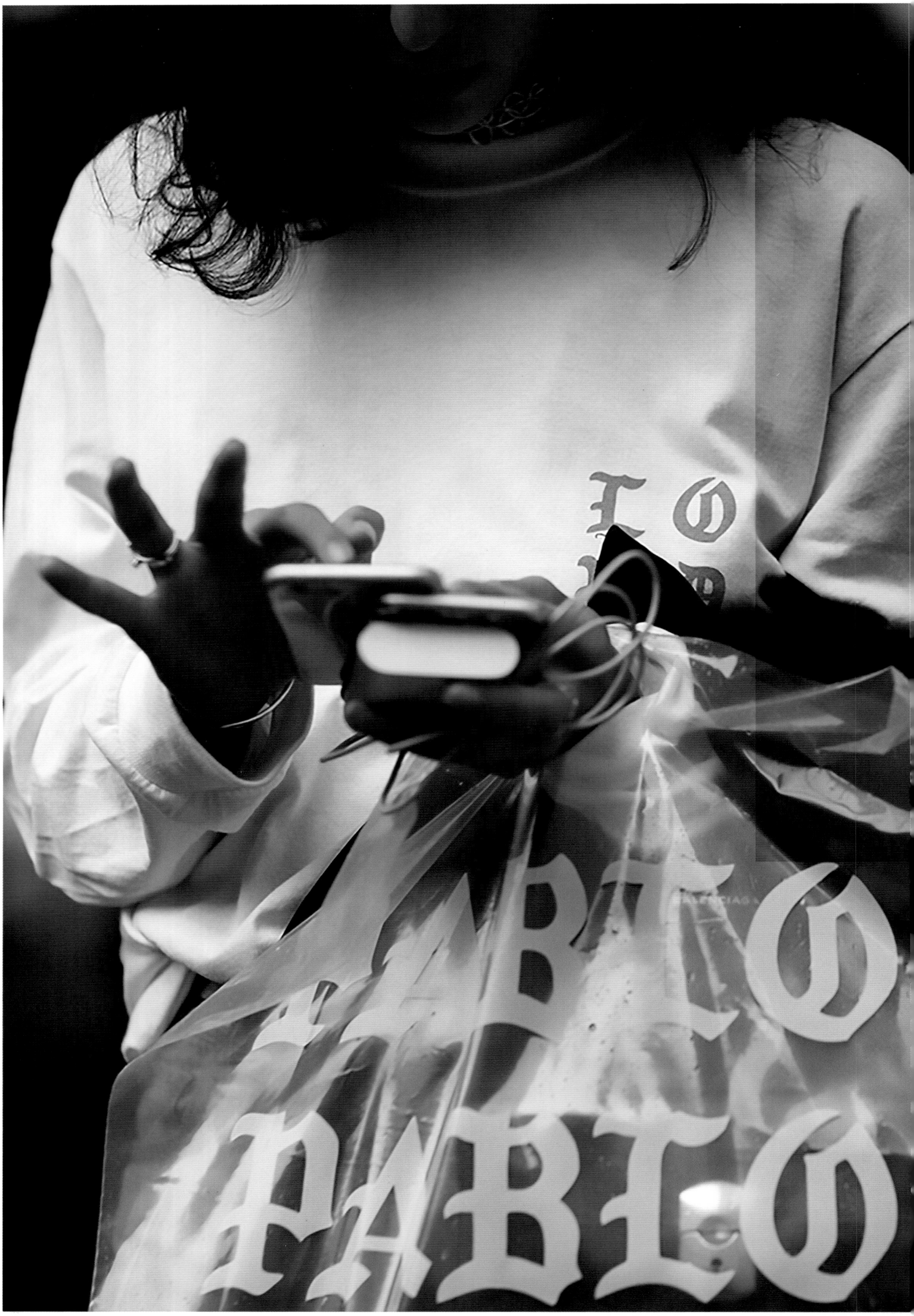
PABLO

165

Author: Byron Hawes
Foreword author: Lawrence Schlossman
Design: Jillian Katz for The Jamais Garde
Photo Manager: Kirsten Chen

Photographers:

Alex Finch / @iamalexfinch
Alexander Robertson / @_arobertson_
Austin Miao / @austinkmiao
Blake Rodich / @blakerodich
Cameron Chen / @camchann
Chris Loutfy / @chrisloutfy
Colin Armstrong / @thecolinarmstrong
Eva Losada / @eva.al.desnudo
Jason T. Lee / @digitalemissions
Liam O'Rourke / @liamxphotography
Niko Pauwels / @npwls_

Page	Date	Location	Brand	Photographer
2	02.11.17	Lyon, France	Yeezy	Niko Pauwels
6	10.17.16	Seoul, South Korea	Vetements	Alex Finch
7	10.17.16	Seoul, South Korea	Vetements	Alex Finch
8	05.13.17	New York, New York	Bathing Ape x Anti Social Social Club	Jason T. Lee
9	05.05.17	New York, New York	Palace	Colin Armstrong
10	05.19.17	New York, New York	Palace	Colin Armstrong
12	08.12.17	London, England	Supreme	Alex Robertson
13	03.16.17	New York, New York	Supreme x Lacoste	Blake Rodich
14	08.15.17	Los Angeles, California	Supreme	Austin Miao
15	08.12.17	London, England	Supreme	Alex Robertson
16	02.11.17	Lyon, France	Yeezy	Niko Pauwels
17	02.11.17	Lyon, France	Yeezy	Niko Pauwels
18	05.05.17	New York, New York	Palace	Colin Armstrong
20	10.17.16	Seoul, South Korea	Vetements	Alex Finch
22	02.11.17	Lyon, France	Yeezy	Niko Pauwels
23	05.13.17	New York, New York	Bathing Ape x Anti Social Social Club	Jason T. Lee
24	05.11.17	London, England	Dover Street Market	Eva Al Desnudo
25	05.13.17	New York, New York	Bathing Ape x Anti Social Social Club	Colin Armstrong
26	10.17.16	Seoul, South Korea	Vetements	Alex Finch
28	10.17.16	Seoul, South Korea	Vetements	Alex Finch
29	02.11.17	Lyon, France	Yeezy	Niko Pauwels
29	10.17.16	Seoul, South Korea	Vetements	Alex Finch
30	05.19.17	New York, New York	Supreme	Colin Armstrong
31	02.11.17	Lyon, France	Yeezy	Niko Pauwels
32	02.11.17	Lyon, France	Yeezy	Niko Pauwels
33	08.20.16	London, England	The Life of Pablo	Eva Al Desnudo
34	10.17.16	Seoul, South Korea	Vetements	Alex Finch
35	08.12.17	London, England	Supreme	Alex Robertson
36	11.25.16	London, England	Palace	Eva Al Desnudo
37	08.16.16	Paris, France	Supreme	Blake Rodich
38	05.05.17	New York, New York	Palace	Colin Armstrong
40	10.17.16	Seoul, South Korea	Vetements	Alex Finch
42	04.28.17	New York, New York	Uniqlo x Kaws	Jason T. Lee
44	08.12.17	London, England	Supreme	Alex Robertson
45	03.16.17	London, England	Supreme x Lacoste	Eva Al Desnudo
45	05.13.17	New York, New York	Bathing Ape x Anti Social Social Club	Jason T. Lee

Page	Date	Location	Brand	Photographer
46	08.16.16	Paris, France	Supreme	Blake Rodich
48	08.12.17	London, England	Supreme	Alex Robertson
49	05.13.17	New York, New York	Bathing Ape x Anti Social Social Club	Colin Armstrong
50	06.30.17	Sydney, Australia	LV x Supreme	Chris Loufty
51	06.30.17	Beijing, China	LV x Supreme	Cameron Chen
53	06.30.17	Sydney, Australia	LV x Supreme	Chris Loufty
54	03.27.17	Shanghai, China	Yuz	Jason T. Lee
55	03.27.17	Shanghai, China	Yuz	Jason T. Lee
56	02.11.17	Lyon, France	Yeezy	Niko Pauwels
57	05.19.17	New York, New York	Palace	Colin Armstrong
58	05.15.17	London, England	Supreme	Liam O'Rourke
59	03.16.17	New York, New York	Supreme x Lacoste	Blake Rodich
60	03.16.17	New York, New York	Supreme x Lacoste	Blake Rodich
61	03.16.17	New York, New York	Supreme x Lacoste	Blake Rodich
62	03.16.17	New York, New York	Supreme x Lacoste	Blake Rodich
64	05.13.17	New York, New York	Bathing Ape x Anti Social Social Club	Jason T. Lee
65	05.13.17	New York, New York	Bathing Ape x Anti Social Social Club	Jason T. Lee
66	06.30.17	Beijing, China	LV x Supreme	Cameron Chen
68	05.19.17	New York, New York	Palace	Colin Armstrong
69	05.19.17	New York, New York	Palace	Colin Armstrong
72	10.17.16	Seoul, South Korea	Vetements	Alex Finch
74	03.25.17	New York, New York	Kinfolk	Blake Rodich
76	05.05.17	New York, New York	Palace	Blake Rodich
77	04.29.17	New York, New York	Rick Owens	Blake Rodich
78	03.16.17	New York, New York	Supreme x Lacoste	Blake Rodich
80	03.16.17	New York, New York	Supreme x Lacoste	Blake Rodich
81	05.19.17	New York, New York	Palace	Colin Armstrong
82	04.06.17	New York, New York	Vlone	Blake Rodich
83	05.19.17	New York, New York	Pop-Up	Colin Armstrong
84	07.18.17	New York, New York	Hype Kills	Colin Armstrong
84	08.16.16	Paris, France	Supreme	Blake Rodich
85	07.18.17	New York, New York	Soho	Colin Armstrong
86	05.05.17	New York, New York	Palace	Blake Rodich
87	04.06.17	New York, New York	Vlone	Blake Rodich
88	08.16.16	Paris, France	Supreme	Blake Rodich

Page	Date	Location	Brand	Photographer
89	05.19.17	New York, New York	Palace	Colin Armstrong
90	04.29.17	New York, New York	Rick Owens	Blake Rodich
91	04.29.17	New York, New York	Rick Owens	Blake Rodich
92	08.16.16	Paris, France	Supreme	Blake Rodich
93	05.15.17	London, England	Supreme	Liam O'Rourke
94	05.19.17	New York, New York	Palace	Colin Armstrong
96	07.18.17	New York, New York	Soho	Colin Armstrong
97	05.19.17	New York, New York	Palace	Colin Armstrong
97	05.19.17	New York, New York	Supreme	Colin Armstrong
98	05.19.17	New York, New York	Palace	Colin Armstrong
100	08.12.17	London, England	Supreme	Alex Robertson
101	03.27.17	Shanghai, China	Yuz Museum x Kaws	Jason T. Lee
102	05.15.17	London, England	Supreme	Liam O'Rourke
103	08.16.16	Paris, France	Supreme	Blake Rodich
104	08.16.16	Paris, France	Supreme	Blake Rodich
105	05.19.17	New York, New York	Palace	Colin Armstrong
106	08.16.16	Paris, France	Supreme	Blake Rodich
107	08.16.16	Paris, France	Supreme	Blake Rodich
108	04.06.17	New York, New York	Vlone	Blake Rodich
109	02.11.17	Lyon, France	Yeezy	Niko Pauwels
110	05.05.17	New York, New York	Palace	Colin Armstrong
110	08.16.16	Paris, France	Supreme	Blake Rodich
111	05.15.17	London, England	Supreme	Liam O'Rourke
112	08.16.16	Paris, France	Supreme	Blake Rodich
114	08.16.16	Paris, France	Supreme	Blake Rodich
115	05.05.17	New York, New York	Palace	Blake Rodich
116	03.16.17	New York, New York	Supreme x Lacoste	Blake Rodich
117	05.05.17	New York, New York	Palace	Blake Rodich
118	05.05.17	New York, New York	Palace	Blake Rodich
119	08.16.16	Paris, France	Supreme	Blake Rodich
119	08.16.16	Paris, France	Supreme	Blake Rodich
121	05.05.17	New York, New York	Palace	Blake Rodich
122	08.16.16	Paris, France	Supreme	Blake Rodich
123	05.05.17	New York, New York	Palace	Colin Armstrong
124	08.16.16	Paris, France	Supreme	Blake Rodich

Page	Date	Location	Brand	Photographer
126	03.16.17	New York, New York	Supreme x Lacoste	Blake Rodich
127	08.16.16	Paris, France	Supreme	Blake Rodich
128	03.16.17	New York, New York	Supreme x Lacoste	Blake Rodich
129	05.13.17	New York, New York	Bape	Jason T. Lee
130	03.16.17	New York, New York	Supreme x Lacoste	Blake Rodich
131	05.05.17	New York, New York	Palace	Colin Armstrong
132	05.05.17	New York, New York	Palace	Blake Rodich
133	03.16.17	New York, New York	Supreme x Lacoste	Blake Rodich
134	05.05.17	New York, New York	Palace	Blake Rodich
135	03.16.17	New York, New York	Supreme x Lacoste	Blake Rodich
136	02.11.17	Lyon, France	Yeezy	Niko Pauwels
138	10.17.16	Seoul, South Korea	Vetements	Alex Finch
139	10.17.16	Seoul, South Korea	Vetements	Alex Finch
140	08.12.17	London, England	Supreme	Alex Robertson
142	10.17.16	Seoul, South Korea	Vetements	Alex Finch
143	05.05.17	New York, New York	Palace	Blake Rodich
144	03.27.17	Shanghai, China	Yuz Museum x Kaws	Jason T. Lee
146	05.05.17	New York, New York	Palace	Colin Armstrong
148	05.05.17	New York, New York	Palace	Colin Armstrong
149	05.19.17	New York, New York	Palace	Jason T. Lee
150	05.05.17	New York, New York	Palace	Colin Armstrong
152	05.05.17	New York, New York	Palace	Colin Armstrong
154	05.05.17	New York, New York	Palace	Blake Rodich
155	05.05.17	New York, New York	Bathing Ape x Anti Social Social Club	Colin Armstrong
156	07.18.17	New York, New York	Supreme	Colin Armstrong
157	06.04.17	New York, New York	Vlone	Blake Rodich
158	06.15.17	New York, New York	Palace	Colin Armstrong
160	05.05.17	New York, New York	Palace	Blake Rodich
162	06.04.17	New York, New York	Vlone	Blake Rodich
163	04.16.17	New York, New York	Nikelab	Colin Armstrong
164	08.20.16	London, England	Pablo	Eva Al Desnudo
165	03.18.17	Tokyo, Japan	Vlone x Fragment Design	Eva Al Desnudo
166	03.27.17	Shanghai, China	Yuz Museum x Kaws	Jason T. Lee
168	05.15.17	London, England	Supreme	Liam O'Rourke

Byron Hawes

Byron Hawes is a New York-based writer and designer. He is the founder and editor of the underground design magazine *The Après Garde,* and co-founder of I-V, a boutique architecture and design firm that has done projects including a recording studio and offices for OVOsound, Campari's Canadian HQ, and Spin Toronto.

He currently serves as contributing editor: architecture and design for *Hypebeast,* and senior editor for *Flofferz,* and was previously a consulting editor at *Architectural Digest China* and Greater China Editor for *BlackBook,* as well as having contributed to publications including *HighSnobiety, Fucking Young!, Monocle, Vice,* and *Wallpaper,* among others.

Additionally, he has authored or co-authored the books *Unbuilt: Conceptual Architecture, We are Wanderful: 25 Years of Design & Fashion in Limburg, Post Industrial Brutalism and the Daiquiri,* and *Modern Tropical: Houses in the Sun.*

Schlossman
Lawrence

Lawrence Schlossman is a fixture in the world of "streetwear" (Ablovian quotations intended) and mens fashion.

From early days handling PR and social media for Mark McNairy to editorial duties at *Complex* to serving as Editor-in-Chief of iconic, and now-defunct, fashion blog-par-excellence Four Pins, Schlossman has been out there creating trends and then dissecting them.

Co-creator and writer of the raucous Tumblr-turned-coffee table book *FuckYeahMensWear,* Schlossman now serves as Brand Director for Grailed.

175

Compilation and editing, text © 2018 Byron Hawes
Photographs © their respective owners and used with permission.
Foreword © 2018 Lawrence Schlossman

Published in the United States by powerHouse Books,
a division of powerHouse Cultural Entertainment, Inc.
32 Adams Street, Brooklyn, NY 11201-1021
e-mail: info@powerHouseBooks.com
website: www.powerHouseBooks.com

First edition, 2018

Library of Congress Control Number: 2018933989

ISBN 978-1-57687-878-1

Printed by: Toppan Leefung

10 9 8 7 6 5 4 3 2 1

Printed and bound in China